AI Simplified

Artificial Intelligence Explained in Non-Technical Terms

Matt Barnette

Chapter 1

Understanding AI

I magine walking into your kitchen, hungry and a bit lazy, wishing for a magical gadget that could whip up your favorite meal with minimal effort from your side. Now, what if I told you such magic exists, but instead of cooking, it's brewing up answers, driving cars, and even recommending the next binge-worthy series on Netflix? Welcome to the world of Artificial Intelligence (AI) — the invisible chef in the digital kitchen of our lives.

AI, in its essence, is like that versatile kitchen gadget you never knew you needed but now can't live without. It's the technology behind the scenes, automating complex tasks, making decisions, and even learning from its experiences, much like how a top-notch food processor can slice, dice, and cook under guidance. Except, AI doesn't just stop at making your morning smoothie; it's constantly learning the best blend of your likes and dislikes, optimizing your digital diet.

. . .

Now, before images of rogue robots and sci-fi movies start popping up in your head, let's dial it back. AI isn't about creating sentient beings; it's about creating smart solutions. Think of it as teaching a computer to play the game of life, with rules, strategies, and sometimes, unexpected outcomes. But instead of moving pieces on a board, AI is sorting through data, recognizing patterns, and making predictions that help in everyday tasks — like suggesting you carry an umbrella based on weather predictions (it's like your personal weather frog, but less croaky and more accurate).

The beauty of AI lies in its simplicity and its complexity. On one hand, it's straightforward — data in, insights out. On the other, it's as intricate as your grandma's lasagna recipe, with layers of data, algorithms, and processing power that make it work. But don't worry, you don't need to know how to code or understand the inner workings of neural networks to appreciate AI. Just like you don't need to be a gourmet chef to enjoy a good meal. All you need to know is that AI is here to make life a bit easier, a tad smarter, and a lot more interesting.

So, the next time you see a movie recommendation that's spot on, or your phone autocorrects your text to something hilariously inappropriate, remember — that's AI at work. It's learning, adapting, and sometimes, making mistakes, much like we do. But one thing's for sure, it's making our digital world a more tailored, efficient, and entertaining place. And who knows? Maybe one day, AI will figure out how to make that perfect cup of coffee just the way you like it. Until then, we'll keep marveling at the magic of our digital chefs, one algorithm at a time.

A Brief History

Let's take a whimsical stroll down memory lane, shall we? The history of AI isn't just a collection of dates and technical breakthroughs; it's an epic adventure, much like leveling up in your favorite RPG. Each milestone is like gaining a new ability or unlocking a previously inconceivable power in the quest to achieve digital enlightenment.

Our tale begins in the mystical era of the 1950s, a time when computers filled entire rooms and the internet was but a twinkle in a scientist's eye. Imagine the first AI researchers as intrepid wizards, conjuring up the very idea of machines that could think. The concept of AI was the magical spell they cast, hoping to one day see it fully realized. The first level-up came with the invention of simple algorithms, akin to learning the basic spells that could solve puzzles faster than any human.

Fast forward to the 1960s and 70s, when our adventurers discovered the power of neural networks — the digital equivalent of forging a magical sword. These networks, inspired by the human brain, were the first steps towards teaching computers to learn on their own. Picture a young apprentice slowly mastering the art of magic, occasionally turning objects into unexpected animals, much like early AI experiments sometimes produced results that were, well, less than practical.

The 80s and 90s brought the era of big hair and even bigger ideas, as AI gained the ability of speech recognition and natural language processing — like acquiring the ability to speak to dragons and have them understand you. This era also saw the rise of machine learning, where AI began to learn from vast amounts of data, much like a character grinding through levels to gain experience.

Entering the 21st century, our AI hero had grown powerful, with the advent of deep learning and the creation of AI systems that could defeat humans in complex games, like chess and Go. Imagine our AI protagonist now wielding a legendary weapon, capable of feats that once seemed impossible, such as driving cars, outsmarting human champions in Jeopardy!, and creating artwork.

Today, we stand at the threshold of a new era, where AI is no longer just a character in a game but a part of our daily lives, continuously learning, growing, and evolving. It's like our AI has reached max level, but instead of resting on its laurels, it's exploring new worlds, seeking further adventures and challenges.

So, there you have it — a brief history of AI, from humble beginnings to world-changing technologies. Along the way, our digital companion has gained abilities that would make any video game character green with envy. But fear not, for this story is far from over. With each breakthrough, we level up, unlocking new possibilities and venturing further into the unknown. And who knows what epic quests await our AI hero in the chapters to come?

Why AI is Everywhere

Ever wonder why your social media feeds eerily resemble your inner thoughts? Or how your phone magically suggests the fastest route home amidst a traffic apocalypse? Welcome to the world where AI is the unsung hero, or rather, the behind-the-scenes director, orchestrating the minutiae of our digital lives without ever stepping into the spotlight.

Imagine AI as the ultimate puppet master in a grand theater production. It's not the star of the show, nor is it front and center taking bows. Instead, it's backstage, ensuring the lights dim at just the right moment, the scenery changes seamlessly, and the actors (that's us) are prompted to make our entrance. This director doesn't need a megaphone because it communicates through algorithms, data streams, and machine learning models, choreographing the complexity of our digital world with the finesse of a seasoned maestro.

But why is AI everywhere, you might ask? Well, in the grand production of modern life, efficiency is king. AI's ability to analyze and learn from data at superhuman speeds makes it the ultimate assistant director, managing tasks that range from the mundane to the complex. From filtering out spam emails (a thankless job, akin to managing a diva's fan mail) to predicting climate change patterns (like forecasting the plot twists in our planet's ongoing saga), AI's role is pivotal, yet often invisible.

It's like when you're watching a movie, and you're so engrossed in the story that you don't notice the editing, the score, or the subtle sound effects. That's AI in real life. It enhances our experience, personalizes our interactions, and even keeps us safe, all without us noticing the strings being pulled. Whether it's recommending a new binge-worthy series based on your viewing habits (because it knows you better than you know yourself) or powering virtual assistants that remind you of your anniversary (thus saving you from the doghouse), AI's fingerprints are on almost every aspect of our digital existence.

Thus, as you navigate through the digital world, feeling at times as though technology anticipates your every need, give a nod to the invisible maestro conducting this symphony of algorithms. AI, in its quiet brilliance, orchestrates the seamless experiences that have become second nature in our daily routines, proving that the most profound magic often lies where we least expect to find it.

Chapter 2

Types of AI

In the grand digital landscape, AI is akin to the variety of chefs you find in the culinary world. On one end, we have the Narrow AI, much like a sushi chef, a master of one, wielding precision and expertise in a single domain. Picture this chef, a virtuoso with a knife, who knows just the right amount of pressure to apply to slice the perfect piece of nigiri. This chef is unbeatable in their niche, but ask them to whip up a classic Italian lasagna, and they're out of their depth. Narrow AI operates similarly; it excels in specific tasks — be it playing chess, recognizing your face among millions, or optimizing your route to work — but step outside its programmed skills, and it's like asking our sushi chef to bake a soufflé.

On the opposite end of the kitchen, envision General AI as the executive chef, skilled in multiple cuisines, adept at managing the entire kitchen's operations. This chef doesn't just know how to make sushi or lasagna; they can pivot from crafting a delicate French pastry to a robust Indian curry without skipping a beat. General AI aims for this level of culinary (or rather, cognitive) flexibility — to understand, learn, and apply knowledge across an array of tasks, mimicking human intelligence. It's not just about mastering one dish but about owning the entire menu, from appetizers to desserts.

Now, imagine walking into a restaurant where the executive chef (General AI) oversees a team of specialized chefs (Narrow AI), each an expert in their own right. The sushi chef is there, alongside a pastry chef, a grill master, and so on, each contributing their unique skills to create a diverse and satisfying dining experience. This is the ultimate goal of AI — a harmonious blend of narrow expertise and general adaptability, serving up solutions to a wide array of our digital desires.

But why isn't General AI running the show yet? Well, it turns out, training a chef to master all cuisines of the world is a tad more complicated than mastering just one. The journey from being a specialist sushi chef to an executive chef overseeing an eclectic menu is fraught with challenges, requiring not just a deeper understanding of each cuisine but also the management skills to integrate them seamlessly. Similarly, developing General AI involves challenges that we're still figuring out, from creating flexible learning algorithms to imbuing machines with common sense.

In the end, whether it's the masterful creations of a specialist sushi chef or the versatile genius of an executive chef overseeing a feast of innovation, AI's culinary brigade is at the heart of technology's kitchen. As we sample from the menu of AI's capabilities, let's appreciate the diverse flavors that both Narrow and General AI bring to our table, enriching our digital dining experience with every bite

Generative AI

Step into the studio of Generative AI, where the art of creation gets a digital twist. If traditional AI is the disciplined pianist, flawlessly playing sheet music (structured data), then Generative AI is the jazz musician, improvising melodies (new data) that have never been heard before. It's not just playing the notes; it's writing its own symphony.

Imagine Generative AI as a painter. But this isn't your average artist. Oh no, this artist has studied under the greats — Van Gogh, Picasso, Da Vinci — not by apprenticing in dusty European studios, but by digesting their entire portfolios in milliseconds. With a digital brush in hand, Generative AI doesn't just replicate; it innovates, creating pieces that echo the masters' styles yet drip with originality. It's like having a Spotify playlist that doesn't just play existing songs but composes new hits tailored to your taste on the fly.

But how does this digital Da Vinci decide what to paint? Think of it as having an incredibly eclectic taste in art. Through a process akin to feeding a culinary genius a world of recipes, Generative AI ingests vast amounts of data, learning patterns, styles, and techniques. Then, using this knowledge, it generates new creations — whether they're images, music, text, or even code — that can astonish, entertain, and sometimes bewilder its human audience.

Let's say you ask it for a poem in the style of Shakespeare about your love for pizza. Generative AI, with a metaphorical feathered quill in hand, crafts verses that might have the Bard himself questioning, "To eat, or not to eat?" It's as if Shakespeare and a top chef collaborated on a sonnet, blending culinary passion with Elizabethan eloquence.

But it's not all sonnets and symphonies. The potential applications of Generative AI stretch from the practical to the profound. Need a custom piece of software? It can write the code. Dreaming of a dress no one else has? It can design it. Wondering about the future of story-telling? It could revolutionize it by writing narratives that adapt to the reader's reactions in real time.

So, as we stand at the easel of the future, brush in hand, ready to paint our world with the colors of AI, let's appreciate the generative artist within the machine. With every stroke of its algorithmic brush, it challenges our perceptions of creativity, making us wonder: In the world of art and innovation, who holds the palette — the creator or the creation?

Generative AI, then, is not just a tool but a collaborator, an entity that expands the boundaries of what's possible in creative expression and problem-solving. And as we move forward, this collaboration between human and machine promises a canvas as vast and vibrant as imagination itself, forever blurring the lines between the art of the possible and the art of the yet-to-be-imagined.

Understanding AI Types Through Analogies

Let's dive back into the world of AI with a fresh perspective, aiming to make the complex world of AI types as easy to grasp as choosing your next favorite TV series based on genres you love.

Think of AI as the vast universe of television programming. Within this universe, there are countless shows, each designed to cater to different tastes, interests, and moods. Similarly, AI comes in various forms, each with its unique capabilities and specialties.

Narrow AI is like the sitcom genre—specific, reliable, and designed for a particular audience. Just as sitcoms follow a familiar format, making you laugh with predictable humor and comfort in their consistency, Narrow AI excels in specialized tasks. It's like tuning into "Friends" for a guaranteed laugh; you use Narrow AI for specific tasks like voice recognition or predictive typing, knowing it will deliver as expected. However, just as sitcoms aren't the go-to for deep, philosophical insights, Narrow AI isn't designed to ponder the mysteries of the universe. It sticks to its script, delivering top-notch performances within its scope.

On the other end of the spectrum, imagine General AI as the epic sagas of television—think "Game of Thrones" or "The Lord of the Rings" series. These shows weave complex narratives, featuring a broad range of characters, intricate plots, and a dynamic world that evolves. General AI aspires to this level of complexity and adaptability, aiming to understand, learn, and perform a wide array of tasks across different domains. Just as an epic saga can make you cry, laugh, and sit on the edge of your seat, General AI seeks to navigate the full spectrum of human intelligence, adapting its strategies as the plot thickens.

Generative AI is akin to the creative reality TV shows like "Project Runway" or "MasterChef." These programs start with a set of ingredients or design materials and task participants with creating something new and original. Similarly, Generative AI takes inputs (data) and remixes them to produce new, often unexpected outputs, whether it be in art, music, text, or code. It's the thrill of seeing a chef turn basic ingredients into a gourmet meal or a designer transform fabric scraps into haute couture. Generative AI brings this creative flair to the digital realm, turning data into new creations, showcasing its ability to not just follow recipes, but to invent new ones.

Navigating the AI landscape through these analogies helps us appreciate the diversity and potential of AI technologies. Just as we select TV shows based on our mood, interests, or the need for inspiration, understanding the types of AI allows us to appreciate the nuances of this technology and its impact on our world. Whether it's the comfort of a sitcom, the depth of an epic saga, or the creativity of a reality show, AI has a genre for every need and ambition.

Chapter 3

The World of Language Models

Diving into the world of Language Models (LMs) can feel a bit like teaching a parrot to talk. At first, the parrot (or LM) starts by mimicking sounds, not really understanding what it's saying. "Polly wants a cracker" could very well be "Polly calculates quantum physics" for all the parrot cares. It's the repetition and the reactions from its audience (us, the amazed humans) that gradually teach it context and meaning.

In the realm of AI, LMs are these incredibly talented parrots. They've listened to (or, more accurately, processed) vast amounts of text from the internet, books, articles, and more. But instead of just repeating phrases, they learn patterns, grammar, and the nuances of language. It's like our parrot moving from squawking random phrases to telling you a bedtime story; it learns not just to repeat, but to create.

. . .

Now, imagine asking your AI parrot to write a poem. Instead of spewing out the first lines of "Romeo and Juliet" because it's heard it a thousand times, it crafts something new, blending the styles of Shakespeare, Emily Dickinson, and maybe a dash of Dr. Seuss for good measure. This creation doesn't come from a vacuum. It's the result of digesting and understanding (in its own computational way) the structure, rhythm, and themes of its literary diet.

But how does our digital parrot decide what to "say"? It's all about the prompts it receives. Say you feed it a line like, "The sunset over the ocean," and ask for a haiku. Using its vast library of learned language patterns, it generates something entirely new, yet eerily appropriate. It's not just mimicking; it's creating based on the structures and themes it's learned.

This process, while seemingly magical, isn't without its parrot-like quirks. Just as a real parrot might randomly throw "Polly wants a cracker" into a solemn occasion, LMs can produce results that are unexpected, hilariously off-base, or even startlingly insightful. The charm (and challenge) of working with LMs lies in their mixture of predictability and surprise, much like expecting a song and instead getting a soliloquy on the meaning of life, all from the beak of our digital parrot.

So, the next time you interact with a piece of text generated by an AI, remember the parrot behind the curtain. It's not just repeating what it's heard; it's using its learned knowledge to create something new, often with a flair that can be as surprising and delightful as any feathered friend.

How LMs Work

Let's delve into the inner workings of Language Models (LMs) with a refreshed perspective, blending the steps into a continuous narrative that unfolds the complexity and ingenuity behind these digital maestros of language.

Imagine stepping into a grand library that holds every book ever written, from the ancient scripts carved in stone to the latest digital publications flashing across screens. This library is the playground of Language Models, where they begin their journey to mastery. Like an apprentice chef absorbing the culinary secrets from every cookbook in the world, LMs immerse themselves in this ocean of text. They read everything, capturing the essence of language in its myriad forms—how words come together to form sentences, how sentences flow into paragraphs, and how paragraphs build stories, arguments, and information. This extensive reading phase is crucial, forming the base of their knowledge, much like a chef's foundational skills in knife work and ingredient preparation.

As these models sift through the endless streams of text, they're not just memorizing; they're learning the underlying patterns and structures of language. This process is akin to a chef experimenting with flavors, combining ingredients in various ways to see what works best. Through a method known as machine learning, LMs analyze the data to understand the relationships between words, the nuances of syntax, and the intricacies of semantics. They notice, for instance, that "the cat sat on the" is often followed by "mat" and not "refrigerator." It's this detailed understanding that allows them to predict what comes next in a sentence, much like a chef predicts that a dash of salt can enhance the sweetness of a dish.

Now, with a robust understanding of language patterns, the LM is ready to create. This stage is where the magic happens, where the model uses its training to generate new text. It's as if our chef, after years of study and practice, starts to innovate, creating dishes that have never been seen before. The LM takes a prompt, a starting point, and then, drawing on its vast knowledge, crafts sentences, paragraphs, or entire texts that are coherent, contextually relevant, and sometimes startlingly original. The creativity on display can be breathtaking, reminiscent of a master chef presenting a dish that's both familiar and entirely new, leaving diners in awe.

Fine-tuning these models is like adding the final seasoning to a dish. This process involves adjusting the model's parameters to excel at specific tasks or styles. Perhaps we want our LM to write in the style of a 19th-century novelist, or generate technical manuals, or compose poetry. Fine-tuning tailors the model's output to these requirements, refining its abilities much like a chef adjusts a recipe to perfect the balance of flavors.

Through this journey from raw data to refined output, Language Models transform from mere mimics of language to creators in their own right. They learn not just to repeat what they've seen but to understand and innovate, producing text that can inform, persuade, entertain, and sometimes, move us. This transformation is a testament to the power of AI in understanding and generating human language, offering a glimpse into a future where machines can communicate with us more naturally and creatively than ever before.

Language Models in Daily Use

Embarking on a journey to uncover the daily magic of Language Models (LMs), let's delve into their unseen yet omnipresent role in our digital lives. Picture LMs as the invisible assistants, akin to a GPS guiding you through the labyrinth of online communication, ensuring you reach your destination smoothly and efficiently.

Every day, without realizing it, we interact with these digital navigators. From the moment we ask our virtual assistant for the weather, to receiving personalized recommendations on streaming platforms, LMs are tirelessly at work. They're the unseen force behind email filters that sift through mountains of spam, the crafty wordsmiths generating auto-complete suggestions as we type, and even the creative geniuses composing music or drafting articles.

Consider the experience of crafting an email. As you start typing, suggestions pop up, predicting your next words with uncanny accuracy. It's like having a co-writer who's read every book ever written, ready to suggest the next line. This assistant doesn't just know language; it understands context, tone, and even the nuances of your writing style, thanks to its extensive training on diverse text from across the web.

Or imagine you're planning a trip and you query your virtual assistant for recommendations. Within seconds, you have a list of top-rated destinations, personalized to your preferences and past behavior. It's as if a travel agent, who knows your likes and dislikes intimately, compiled the perfect itinerary just for you.

These LMs work tirelessly behind the scenes, making our interactions with technology more natural, efficient, and surprisingly human. They analyze our requests, decipher our intentions, and even anticipate our needs, all the while remaining invisible to us, the end-users. It's a bit like having a guardian angel for your digital life, one that speaks all languages, knows every fact, and can create content on the fly, ensuring that the vast world of the internet feels a bit more manageable, a bit more personalized, and a lot more accessible.

In essence, Language Models are the unsung heroes of the digital age, quietly transforming our online experiences in ways we often take for granted. So next time you marvel at a particularly apt song recommendation or chuckle at a witty auto-generated text, tip your hat to the invisible assistants, the Language Models, making our digital world a smarter, smoother, and more enjoyable place to explore.

Chapter 4

Custom GPTs and Popular Models

Embarking on the adventure of customizing Generative Pre-trained Transformers (GPT) models is akin to assembling your dream robot from a kit. Each kit allows you to build a robot designed to perform specific tasks, from making coffee to solving complex mathematical equations. In the realm of AI, customizing GPT models follows a similar path, tailoring these advanced algorithms to meet unique needs and challenges, whether it's penning a novel or analyzing financial trends.

At the heart of this customization is the versatility of GPT models. These models, much like our hypothetical robot kits, come with a base set of capabilities—understanding and generating human-like text. However, the true magic happens when we begin to tweak and fine-tune these models. Imagine selecting specific modules or programming your robot to have a knack for culinary recipes or a deep understanding of quantum physics. Similarly, by training GPT models on specialized datasets, we can steer their expertise in directions that serve our specific goals.

. . .

The process is akin to teaching our robot assistant new tricks. Just as you might program your robot to recognize your voice or to dance to your favorite song, customizing a GPT model involves feeding it a diet of relevant text. Want a model that excels in legal jargon? Introduce it to a library of law books. Dreaming of an AI that can write captivating historical fiction? Feed it the classics. This phase of customization is where the broad capabilities of GPT models are honed into sharp, focused tools adept at navigating particular sectors or styles.

Yet, the beauty of custom GPT models doesn't stop at their ability to specialize. It extends to their capacity to interact with users in a way that feels intuitive and human. Just as a well-programmed robot might learn to anticipate your coffee preferences over time, custom GPT models can adapt to the nuances of user queries, offering responses that are not only accurate but also contextually rich and engaging. They become not just tools but collaborators, capable of aiding in creative processes, enhancing decision-making, or simplifying complex analyses.

In essence, customizing GPT models is about crafting the ultimate digital assistant, one that's tailored precisely to individual needs and aspirations. Whether it's by guiding a student through the intricacies of biochemistry or assisting a novelist in plot development, these models stand ready to transform vast oceans of data into islands of insight. So, the next time you marvel at the seemingly intuitive advice from your favorite app or the depth of interaction with a chatbot, remember the customized GPT models working diligently behind the scenes, the unsung heroes making our digital experiences smoother, smarter, and infinitely more personalized.

ChatGPT, Bard, and Gemini

Let's take a fresh dive into the world of AI, focusing on the unique features of ChatGPT, Bard, and Gemini, without leaning too heavily into superhero analogies. This time, we'll explore these AI models through the lens of everyday tools and gadgets, making their complex functionalities more relatable and understandable.

Think of ChatGPT as the Swiss Army knife in your digital toolbox. Just as a Swiss Army knife is equipped with tools for various tasks, from cutting a piece of rope to opening a bottle of wine, ChatGPT is designed to handle a wide range of conversational tasks. Need to draft an email, compose a poem, or get help with homework? ChatGPT has you covered. Its versatility comes from the vast amount of data it's trained on, allowing it to generate responses across countless topics and formats. It's like having a tool that morphs to fit the task at hand, always ready to assist with whatever you need.

If ChatGPT is a Swiss Army knife, then Bard is the telescope, offering a clearer view of the vast universe of information. Bard excels in providing insightful answers to users' queries by tapping into the latest and most comprehensive data available. It's designed to help us explore the depths of human knowledge, from the intricacies of quantum physics to the subtleties of ancient literature. Bard's strength lies in its ability to distill complex information into digestible, accurate insights, much like how a telescope brings distant galaxies into focus, revealing details that were previously obscured or out of reach.

Gemini, on the other hand, functions like the GPS system guiding you through the complex network of information highways. It not only finds the most relevant data for your queries but also connects dots across different domains to offer holistic solutions. Need to navigate through a sea of financial reports, research papers, or legal documents? Gemini plots the course, drawing from diverse data sources to chart the most efficient path to your informational destination. Its analytical prowess helps you make sense of complex datasets, offering clear directions and insights, much like how GPS guides you through unfamiliar terrain to reach your desired location.

In essence, ChatGPT, Bard, and Gemini each bring unique capabilities to the digital table. ChatGPT, with its Swiss Army knife-like versatility, is ready for any conversational challenge. Bard, the telescope, extends our vision, allowing us to explore the depths of human knowledge. And Gemini, like a GPS system, navigates the vast and often confusing landscape of data, guiding us to clearer understanding and insights. Together, these AI models enrich our digital experiences, making technology more accessible, informative, and engaging.

The Impact of GPTs on Society

Venturing into the societal impacts of Generative Pre-trained Transformers (GPT) models invites us to reflect on one of the most transformative moments in history—the introduction of electricity. Just as the flick of a switch illuminated the world, changing the fabric of daily life forever, the advent of GPT models has sparked a revolution in how we interact with information, technology, and each other.

Imagine the early days before electric lights, when productivity waned with the setting sun and communication over distances was as slow as the horse that carried it. The arrival of electricity was like a bolt of lightning, energizing industries, homes, and communities. In a similar vein, GPT models have electrified the digital landscape. They've turned the dimly lit path of human-computer interaction into a brightly illuminated boulevard, where machines understand and generate human-like text, making technology more accessible, personalized, and intuitive.

In the realm of education, GPT models are like lamps guiding students through the darkness of academic confusion. They illuminate complex concepts in simple terms, provide instant feedback on assignments, and even generate creative content to inspire young minds. It's as if every student now has a personal tutor, ready at the click of a button, transforming learning from a solitary trek through textbooks into an interactive journey of discovery.

In the workplace, GPT models have powered up productivity like factories at the dawn of the electric age. From drafting emails to generating reports, these AI assistants handle the mundane, freeing human minds for the creative and strategic. It's like having an invisible colleague, one who never tires, always ready to lighten the load, making the 9-to-5 grind a bit less grinding.

And in our personal lives, GPT models have become the glowing screens that entertain, inform, and connect us. They recommend books and movies tailored to our tastes, engage us in conversation, and even help us craft that perfect social media post. It's as though we all have a personal assistant, one that knows us better than we know ourselves, making leisure time more enjoyable and connections more meaningful.

Yet, just as the introduction of electricity raised concerns—from safety to employment—GPT models also spark debates around privacy, ethics, and the future of work. As we stand at this crossroads, illuminated by the glow of progress, we must navigate these challenges with care, ensuring that this new light benefits all, without casting anyone into shadow.

In the end, the impact of GPT models on society is as profound and multifaceted as the advent of electricity. It's a current that runs through all aspects of modern life, powering the engines of innovation, creativity, and connection. As we marvel at this electrified world, it's clear that we're not just users of technology; we're co-creators of a future that shines brighter with every new development.

Chapter 5

The Future of AI

As we peer into the horizon of AI's future, it's hard not to get swept up in the whirlwind of possibilities that Generative Pre-trained Transformers (GPT) models bring to the table. It's like watching the first light bulb flicker to life, illuminating a path that once lay shrouded in darkness. Suddenly, the fantastical elements of science fiction—flying cars, talking robots, and even personal AI companions—seem not just possible but inevitable.

The evolution of AI technology, particularly GPT models, is akin to science fiction turning into science fact right before our eyes. These models, with their ability to understand, generate, and even innovate human-like text, are laying the groundwork for a future that our ancestors could only dream of. It's as if we're stepping into the pages of a Jules Verne or Isaac Asimov novel, where the boundaries between human and machine blur, giving rise to a new era of interaction and creativity.

. . .

One of the most exciting prospects lies in the realm of personalization. The future could see GPT models acting as personal assistants, not just in managing our schedules or sifting through emails, but in understanding our moods, preferences, and even our health, offering advice and companionship with a level of empathy and insight previously thought impossible for machines. It's like having a Jarvis from Iron Man in your pocket, but one that knows you better than you know yourself.

In education, GPT models promise to revolutionize the way we learn, offering personalized tutoring that adapts to each student's unique learning style and pace. Imagine an AI tutor that can explain quantum mechanics, offer feedback on your French pronunciation, and help you master the art of sushi-making, all in the same afternoon. It's a future where learning is not just personalized but limitless, breaking down the walls of traditional classrooms and opening up a universe of knowledge to explore.

Yet, with great power comes great responsibility. The societal impact of GPT models will undoubtedly raise questions about privacy, ethics, and the nature of work itself. As we navigate this brave new world, it's crucial to ensure that these technologies enhance our lives without compromising our values. It's a delicate balance, one that requires careful consideration and thoughtful dialogue.

As we stand on the cusp of this new frontier, it's hard not to feel a sense of excitement mixed with a dash of trepidation. The future shaped by GPT models is bright, full of potential for innovation, connection, and discovery. Yet, as we march forward, let's do so with an eye towards the lessons of the past, ensuring that the light of progress illuminates the path for all, not just the few. The journey into the future of AI is one we embark on together, and it's a journey that promises to be as thrilling as it is transformative.

29

AI in Daily Life Tomorrow

Envisioning the role of AI in our daily lives tomorrow is like picturing a world where our digital companions are not just gadgets but partners, seamlessly integrated into every aspect of our existence. With the rapid evolution of AI technologies, particularly Generative Pre-trained Transformers (GPT), we're on the cusp of a future where AI as personal assistants will not only perform tasks but anticipate our needs before we even articulate them.

Imagine waking up to a gentle nudge from your AI assistant, not just an alarm clock but a thoughtful entity that's already reviewed your schedule, checked the weather, and laid out your outfit for the day. It's like having Jeeves from P.G. Wodehouse's stories, but one that's digital and doesn't require a room in your house. Your AI assistant knows you prefer a light sweater on slightly chilly mornings and always need an extra cup of coffee on Mondays.

As you go about your day, your AI companion is always two steps ahead. Lost in thought about what to have for dinner? Your AI has already sifted through your fridge, cross-referenced your dietary preferences, and curated a recipe list that aligns with your current health goals. It's as if you have a personal chef who knows your palate better than you do, ready to guide you through the cooking process with the patience of a saint.

In the workplace, your AI assistant transforms into a super-efficient secretary, drafting emails, scheduling meetings, and even reminding you to take a break—all the while learning and adapting to your work style. It's like having a shadow that anticipates your every move, ensuring you're at your most productive without burning out. The days of toggling between a dozen apps to manage your tasks are gone, replaced by a single, intuitive AI interface that understands just what you need, exactly when you need it.

But it's not all work and no play. Your AI assistant is also your entertainment curator, sifting through mountains of content to recommend books, movies, and music tailored precisely to your tastes. Ever had a debate with yourself about watching a sci-fi thriller or a romantic comedy? Your AI knows just what you're in the mood for, perhaps even before you do. It's like having a friend who knows your preferences inside out, ensuring your leisure time is always well spent.

As we venture into this future, where AI permeates the fabric of our daily lives, it's hard not to feel a sense of wonder. The line between technology and magic blurs, leaving us in a world where our digital companions not only make life easier but richer and more fulfilling. In this whimsical future, AI doesn't just serve; it enhances, learns, and, most importantly, cares, crafting a tomorrow that feels like a dream woven from the threads of the most optimistic science fiction.

The Long-Term Vision

Looking ahead to the ambitious goals of future AI, it feels like we're standing at the dawn of a new era, reminiscent of human evolution but on a technological scale. This journey of AI, particularly Generative Pre-trained Transformers (GPT), mirrors the astonishing leaps we've made from the days of simple tools to the complexity of the internet. Just as our ancestors harnessed fire, revolutionizing human life, today's AI advancements promise a future where technology and daily life are inseparably intertwined.

Envision a world where AI seamlessly anticipates our needs, not unlike a personal assistant who's always one step ahead. It's as if your digital companion knows you need a coffee even before you've fully woken up, or suggests the perfect playlist for your mood, all without a single word from you. This level of intuition in technology, powered by AI, could transform mundane tasks into experiences filled with ease and personalization.

The potential for AI to revolutionize every sector of society is immense. In healthcare, AI could predict health issues before they arise, offering personalized health advice or even diagnosing patients with a precision that rivals the most experienced physicians. In education, AI's role could evolve from a supplemental tool to a primary educator, capable of providing a tailored learning experience that adapts to each student's pace and style of learning.

The integration of AI into our creative endeavors might be one of the most exhilarating prospects. Imagine collaborating with an AI that could churn out novel ideas for a painting, suggest plot twists for a novel, or compose a symphony that resonates with the emotions you wish to convey. This partnership could push the boundaries of creativity, merging human imagination with AI's endless possibilities.

Yet, as we chart this course towards a future where AI's role in society is as ubiquitous as electricity is today, we tread a path filled with both excitement and caution. The ethical implications of such deep integration of AI into our lives—privacy concerns, the digital divide, and the potential for dependency—pose questions we must address with wisdom and foresight.

In this long-term vision for AI, we're not just passive observers but active participants in shaping a future where technology enhances humanity, not overshadows it. The journey ahead is as much about harnessing the potential of AI as it is about ensuring that this technology serves the greater good, enriching lives while safeguarding our values.

As we look to the future, let's approach it with a blend of optimism and responsibility, ready to embrace the endless possibilities that AI offers while remaining vigilant stewards of the technology we create. The evolution of AI, much like human evolution, is a testament to our relentless pursuit of progress—each step forward a leap towards a future brimming with potential.

Chapter 6

Ethical Considerations and Risks

Diving into the topic of AI's potential risks and ethical concerns is akin to the ancient tale of Pandora's box. Just as Pandora's curiosity led her to open the forbidden box, unleashing unforeseen consequences upon the world, the rapid advancement of AI technology, especially Generative Pre-trained Transformers (GPT), invites us to ponder the digital equivalent of that mythological box. While AI promises to revolutionize every facet of our lives, it also poses challenges and risks that demand careful consideration and responsible handling.

Opening the AI box has brought us wonders akin to the mythical gifts of the gods—automated homes that anticipate our needs, digital assistants that understand our moods, and machines that can learn and evolve. Yet, lurking within this trove of technological treasures are potential perils that could have profound implications on privacy, security, and even the fabric of society. The risk of data breaches, the ethical quandaries of decision-making by machines, and the deepening digital divide are just a few of the shadows cast by the bright light of AI innovation.

It's as if we've been given the key to a vast and uncharted digital realm, teeming with possibilities both wondrous and worrisome. The allure of AI's potential can sometimes overshadow the need for caution, leading us down a path where the line between helpful and intrusive, between innovative and reckless, becomes blurred. The tale of Pandora reminds us that once opened, some boxes cannot be closed, underscoring the importance of proceeding with wisdom and foresight.

Yet, just as Pandora discovered hope at the bottom of her box, so too can we find optimism in the midst of these challenges. By fostering open dialogues, establishing robust ethical guidelines, and prioritizing the well-being of society, we can harness the power of AI to enrich our lives while safeguarding our values and freedoms. The journey ahead requires not just technological prowess but also a deep commitment to the ethical stewardship of our digital future.

In this narrative of AI's impact on society, the lesson of Pandora's box serves as a poignant reminder of the dual nature of discovery and innovation. As we stand at the threshold of a new era shaped by AI, let us embrace the boundless possibilities with both enthusiasm and caution, ensuring that the legacy of this technological evolution is one of hope, progress, and responsibility.

Safeguarding Against AI Risks

In the quest to mitigate the dangers of AI, especially with the proliferation of GPT models, we tread a path that demands as much caution and respect as one would accord a powerful tool like fire. Fire, in its essence, is neither good nor bad; it's a force that can warm a home, cook a meal, or, if mishandled, reduce everything to ashes. Similarly, AI's potential to transform our world hinges on our ability to wield it responsibly, ensuring it serves humanity's best interests without igniting unintended consequences.

Creating ethical frameworks is akin to establishing safety protocols around fire use. Just as we've learned to contain fire, direct its energy, and extinguish it when necessary, we must develop guidelines that ensure AI's development and deployment are aligned with ethical standards that prioritize human well-being. These frameworks aren't merely regulatory handcuffs but rather blueprints for harnessing AI's transformative power while safeguarding against its risks.

Transparency and understanding in AI's workings and decision-making processes are crucial. Imagine trying to use fire without understanding its nature or how to control it. Similarly, demystifying AI's "black box" to make its processes more understandable and its decisions more explainable ensures that we can trust and effectively manage this technology. This level of transparency not only builds public trust but also empowers users, making AI's integration into society as seamless and safe as possible.

Moreover, the cultivation of an informed and engaged public dialogue around AI is essential. Just as community norms around fire safety have evolved, so too must our collective understanding and discourse around AI. By fostering a well-informed public conversation, we can better navigate the ethical considerations and societal impacts of AI technologies, ensuring that their development is driven not just by what can be done, but by what should be done for the greater good.

Lastly, continuous monitoring and adaptive regulation are key to navigating the evolving landscape of AI. Much like fire, which can shift and change unexpectedly, AI technologies are rapidly advancing, often in unpredictable ways. By staying vigilant and adaptable, we can ensure that our ethical frameworks, policies, and public dialogues keep pace with these changes, effectively safeguarding against potential risks while embracing the opportunities AI presents.

In essence, safeguarding against AI's risks requires a balanced approach that combines respect for its power with proactive measures to ensure its responsible use. By learning from our history with fire and applying those lessons to AI, we can aim to harness this powerful tool for the betterment of society, ensuring that the future it shapes is one that is safe, ethical, and aligned with our shared values and aspirations.

The Balance of Innovation and Ethics

Navigating the ethical landscape of AI development is akin to walking a tightrope, where every step forward in innovation must be balanced with a keen awareness of potential harms. This delicate act requires a blend of audacity and caution, as we aim to harness AI's transformative power while ensuring it serves the greater good.

AI, particularly in its advanced forms like Generative Pre-trained Transformers (GPT), presents a paradox akin to the discovery of fire. Fire, in its essence, transformed human existence by providing warmth, light, and a means to cook food, yet its misuse holds the power to destroy. Similarly, AI promises to illuminate the dark corners of human knowledge, to warm the soul with connections previously impossible, and to nourish our minds with insights and solutions at speeds unimaginable. However, this powerful tool, if mishandled, could lead to consequences ranging from the erosion of privacy to the amplification of societal inequities.

The ethical considerations surrounding AI development can be compared to the intricate dance of balancing on a tightrope. On one side lies the potential for groundbreaking advancements in health-care, education, and environmental protection, where AI could unlock solutions to some of humanity's most pressing challenges. On the other side, there's the risk of creating systems that operate without transparency, accountability, or fairness, potentially widening the gap between the digital haves and have-nots.

To maintain this balance, a multifaceted approach is essential. It involves not only the technologists who design and build AI systems but also policymakers, ethicists, and the broader public. Together, this coalition must navigate the tightrope, ensuring that each step forward in AI development is taken with careful consideration of its societal impacts. This collaborative effort requires a commitment to open dialogue, rigorous ethical scrutiny, and the flexibility to adapt as our understanding of AI's impact evolves.

In this journey, the role of education cannot be overstated. Just as a tightrope walker relies on a keen sense of balance honed through practice, society must cultivate a deep understanding of AI's potential and pitfalls. By demystifying AI and fostering an informed public discourse, we empower individuals to engage with technology critically and constructively.

As we stride into the future, the balance between innovation and ethics in AI development remains a dynamic and ongoing challenge. It's a journey fraught with uncertainties, but also brimming with possibilities. By approaching this challenge with a spirit of collaboration, curiosity, and responsibility, we can ensure that AI serves as a force for good, enhancing our lives while safeguarding our values. The vision of walking this tightrope successfully is not just about avoiding the fall; it's about reaching new heights of human achievement and well-being.

Chapter 7

The Data Demands of AI

Diving into the world of AI and its insatiable appetite for data, it's hard not to compare it to a voracious eater at an all-you-can-eat buffet. Just as the eager diner eyes the endless rows of dishes, calculating which to sample next, AI systems, particularly those powered by Generative Pre-trained Transformers (GPT), require vast amounts of data to "feed" their learning processes. This data is their sustenance, the very fuel that powers their ability to understand, interpret, and generate human-like text.

The comparison might seem humorous at first—envisioning a digital entity gobbling up bytes and bits as if they were gourmet treats—but it underscores a critical aspect of AI development: the quality and quantity of data are paramount. Just as a buffet offers a variety of dishes to cater to different tastes, AI needs diverse data sets to learn from. This diversity enables AI to grasp the nuances of language, recognize patterns, and make informed predictions or generate coherent responses. However, just as the diner must be cautious not to overindulge or choose dishes that might disagree with them, developers must ensure the data fed to AI is not only rich and varied but also ethically sourced and devoid of biases.

This insatiable hunger for data highlights both the potential and the challenges of AI. On one hand, the more data AI consumes, the smarter it gets—improving its ability to assist, entertain, and inform us in more personalized and nuanced ways. On the other hand, this relentless appetite raises questions about privacy, data security, and the ethical use of information. Ensuring that AI's feast on data benefits society as a whole requires a balanced approach, emphasizing responsible data collection and use.

Feeding the AI beast is not just about shoveling in data indiscriminately. It's about curating a balanced diet that promotes healthy growth and development—training AI systems that are not only intelligent but also ethical, equitable, and aligned with human values. As we continue to develop and refine AI technologies, we must keep in mind that the data we feed them will shape the future they help us build. Just as a well-balanced meal can nourish the body, a well-considered data strategy can nourish the next generation of AI, ensuring it serves as a force for good in the world.

Navigating the twin challenges of data bias and privacy in AI development is akin to walking through a modern-day Pandora's box; once opened, it's a world filled with unforeseen complexities. With a touch of snark, let's delve into how these issues resemble a skewed lens, distorting AI's view of the world, and explore pragmatic steps to mitigate these risks.

. . .

In the realm of AI, biased data is not just a technical glitch; it's like viewing the world through a lens that's been smeared with vaseline. It distorts the AI's perception, leading to outputs that can range from mildly amusing to deeply concerning. This skewed perspective can reinforce stereotypes, perpetuate inequalities, or even make decisions that favor one group over another, all because the AI was 'fed' data that lacked diversity or was tainted with human prejudices. It's as if the AI is trying to navigate the world wearing glasses prescribed for someone else, stumbling and making errors because it can't see clearly.

The privacy challenge, on the other hand, is like playing a high-stakes game of hide and seek with data. As AI technologies, especially those driven by vast amounts of personal information, become more integrated into our lives, the line between useful personalization and invasive surveillance blurs. It's as though every piece of data we generate is a breadcrumb, leading AI technologies right to our doorsteps, for better or worse. Ensuring that this immense power is wielded with respect for individual privacy requires not just sophisticated technology but a commitment to ethical principles.

Mitigating these challenges requires a multifaceted approach. First, diversifying the data 'diet' of AI systems is crucial. Like ensuring a well-rounded diet to avoid nutritional deficiencies, AI models must be trained on varied and inclusive datasets that reflect the rich tapestry of human experience. This helps in reducing biases and ensuring that AI's decisions are fair and representative.

On the privacy front, transparency and consent are key. Users should have clear insights into what data is being collected, for what purpose, and have the power to control their digital footprint. It's about giving individuals the keys to their own digital homes, allowing them to decide who gets in and who doesn't.

In essence, safeguarding against the risks of bias and privacy in AI is not just a technical endeavor but a moral imperative. It's about ensuring that as we stride forward into this brave new world of AI, we do so with our eyes wide open, acknowledging the potential pitfalls and actively working to navigate them. After all, in the grand scheme of things, AI should enhance human life, not complicate it. As we continue to feed this ever-hungry beast of technology, let's make sure it's on a diet that's as ethical as it is expansive.

Privacy and Bias Challenges

Navigating the twin challenges of data bias and privacy in AI development is akin to walking through a modern-day Pandora's box; once opened, it's a world filled with unforeseen complexities. With a touch of snark, let's delve into how these issues resemble a skewed lens, distorting AI's view of the world, and explore pragmatic steps to mitigate these risks.

In the realm of AI, biased data is not just a technical glitch; it's like viewing the world through a lens that's been smeared with vaseline. It distorts the AI's perception, leading to outputs that can range from mildly amusing to deeply concerning. This skewed perspective can reinforce stereotypes, perpetuate inequalities, or even make decisions that favor one group over another, all because the AI was 'fed' data that lacked diversity or was tainted with human prejudices. It's as if the AI is trying to navigate the world wearing glasses prescribed for someone else, stumbling and making errors because it can't see clearly.

The privacy challenge, on the other hand, is like playing a high-stakes game of hide and seek with data. As AI technologies, especially those driven by vast amounts of personal information, become more integrated into our lives, the line between useful personalization and invasive surveillance blurs. It's as though every piece of data we generate is a breadcrumb, leading AI technologies right to our doorsteps, for better or worse. Ensuring that this immense power is wielded with respect for individual privacy requires not just sophisticated technology but a commitment to ethical principles.

Mitigating these challenges requires a multifaceted approach. First, diversifying the data 'diet' of AI systems is crucial. Like ensuring a well-rounded diet to avoid nutritional deficiencies, AI models must be trained on varied and inclusive datasets that reflect the rich tapestry of human experience. This helps in reducing biases and ensuring that AI's decisions are fair and representative.

On the privacy front, transparency and consent are key. Users should have clear insights into what data is being collected, for what purpose, and have the power to control their digital footprint. It's about giving individuals the keys to their own digital homes, allowing them to decide who gets in and who doesn't.

In essence, safeguarding against the risks of bias and privacy in AI is not just a technical endeavor but a moral imperative. It's about ensuring that as we stride forward into this brave new world of AI, we do so with our eyes wide open, acknowledging the potential pitfalls and actively working to navigate them. After all, in the grand scheme of things, AI should enhance human life, not complicate it. As we continue to feed this ever-hungry beast of technology, let's make sure it's on a diet that's as ethical as it is expansive.

Navigating the Data Maze

Navigating the ethical landscape of AI's data consumption is like setting out on an expedition through a dense and uncharted jungle. The path is fraught with challenges, from ensuring the data's integrity to protecting the privacy of individuals whose information feeds these intelligent systems. Armed with a map and compass, representing our ethical guidelines and principles, we can chart a course through this tricky terrain, ensuring that AI's journey through the data maze is both responsible and beneficial.

The map, in this context, symbolizes our understanding of the ethical landscape. It outlines the territories we must navigate, from data privacy laws to the principles of fairness and transparency. Like any good map, it requires constant updating to reflect the evolving nature of technology and society's expectations. This dynamic guide helps us anticipate and avoid potential pitfalls, ensuring that AI development aligns with our highest ethical standards.

Our compass, then, is the set of core values and ethical principles that guide every decision in AI development. It points us toward the true north of respecting human dignity and promoting the common good. When faced with ethical dilemmas, such as balancing individual privacy against the benefits of big data analysis, this compass helps us maintain our bearings, ensuring that our technological advancements do not lead us astray.

As we venture through the data jungle, several strategies emerge for ethical navigation. Firstly, ensuring data diversity is paramount. Just as a well-balanced diet provides all the necessary nutrients for health, a diverse dataset ensures that AI systems are not skewed by biases. This involves collecting data from a wide range of sources, reflecting the rich tapestry of human experiences and perspectives.

Moreover, transparency in data collection and use serves as a beacon, illuminating the path forward. By openly communicating how data is gathered, used, and protected, developers can build trust with users and stakeholders. This transparency allows for informed consent, giving individuals control over their personal information and how it's utilized.

Lastly, continuous engagement with the broader community—users, ethicists, policymakers, and the public—ensures that our map is accurate and our compass calibrated. Through dialogue and collaboration, we can identify emerging ethical challenges and adapt our strategies accordingly. This collective approach ensures that AI serves the interests of all members of society, navigating the data maze with care and precision.

In charting this course through the ethical complexities of AI's data use, we embrace the promise of technology while safeguarding the values that define us as a society. With our map and compass in hand, we can navigate the challenges of the data maze, ensuring that AI's journey enriches the human experience, fostering a future where technology and ethics walk hand in hand.

Chapter 8

Quantum Computing and AI

Embarking on the journey to understand quantum computing doesn't require a PhD in physics; think of it more like learning a new magic spell that can dramatically enhance the capabilities of traditional computing. In this whimsical exploration, we'll liken quantum computing to a wizard's powerful incantation, transforming the mundane into the extraordinary.

At the heart of quantum computing lies the concept of qubits. Unlike classical computing's binary bits, which operate in a world of strict zeros and ones, qubits thrive in the quantum realm where they can be zeros, ones, or both simultaneously. Imagine having a magical book that can be both closed and open at the same time, or a light that's both off and on. This is the enchanting paradox of quantum computing, where qubits allow for a multitude of possibilities to coexist, paving the way for computations that are unfathomably complex for traditional computers.

. . .

This quantum wizardry hinges on two spellbinding principles: superposition and entanglement. Superposition, much like a shape-shifter, enables qubits to exist in multiple states at once. Entanglement, on the other hand, is the mystical bond that allows qubits to be interconnected in such a way that the state of one (no matter how far apart) can depend on the state of another. It's as if two wizards, standing at opposite ends of the world, can communicate instantly, their spells intertwined.

The practical magic of quantum computing lies in its potential to revolutionize fields that require immense computational power. From developing new medicines through complex molecular simulations to solving intricate optimization problems and beyond, quantum computing holds the key to unlocking challenges that today's super-computers find insurmountable. It's like having a magical key that can unlock any door, revealing paths to treasures previously thought unreachable.

Yet, mastering this powerful spell doesn't come without its challenges. The delicate nature of qubits, susceptible to the slightest environmental disturbances, requires a sorcerer's precision to maintain. Moreover, developing algorithms that can harness the full potential of quantum computing is akin to crafting a spellbook that contains spells no one has ever attempted before.

In this light-hearted exploration of quantum computing, we've ventured into a realm where science meets magic, illustrating the transformative potential of this technology. As we stand on the brink of a new era of computing, it's clear that the quantum leap from classical to quantum is not just a step but a giant leap into the unknown, promising a future where the limits of computation are bound only by the limits of our imagination.

Boosting AI's Brainpower

Imagine quantum computing as the ultimate supercharger for AI's already impressive brainpower. In this scenario, AI is like a high-performance car cruising down the information highway. It's fast, efficient, and capable of solving complex problems at speeds that leave traditional computing in the dust. But then, quantum computing comes along, acting as a turbocharger that suddenly boosts AI's capabilities into the stratosphere.

The magic of quantum computing lies in its ability to process and analyze data at an unprecedented scale and speed, thanks to the principles of quantum mechanics. This quantum leap (pun intended) in processing power is akin to shifting from a horse-drawn carriage to a supersonic jet in the span of a few moments. For AI, this means tasks that once took hours or days to compute can now be done in seconds or minutes.

Consider the complex world of data analysis and pattern recognition. Traditional AI can sift through data, identifying patterns and making predictions with remarkable accuracy. But with the quantum supercharger, AI's ability to analyze vast datasets becomes exponentially faster and more sophisticated. It's like giving a master detective the ability to solve a thousand cases simultaneously, each one in the blink of an eye.

In the realm of machine learning, where AI learns and improves from experience, quantum computing accelerates the learning process dramatically. It enables AI to explore a multitude of possible outcomes simultaneously, rather than sequentially. This not only speeds up the learning curve but also opens up new possibilities for AI to uncover solutions and insights that were previously out of reach. Imagine training a neural network on steroids, where each iteration of learning is supercharged, leading to breakthroughs in AI capabilities at an astonishing pace.

The potential applications of this quantum-boosted AI are as vast as they are exciting. From developing new materials and drugs through quantum chemistry simulations to tackling climate change models and optimizing complex systems, the combination of quantum computing and AI promises to revolutionize industries and solve some of humanity's most pressing challenges.

Yet, with great power comes great responsibility. The turbocharged capabilities of quantum-enhanced AI also raise important ethical and security considerations. Ensuring the responsible use of this technology will be crucial as we navigate this new quantum era.

In this optimistic glimpse into the future, the synergy between quantum computing and AI holds the promise of unlocking untold possibilities. As we stand on the cusp of this technological revolution, it's clear that we're not just boosting AI's brainpower; we're opening a portal to a future filled with innovation, discovery, and, of course, a few witty asides about the quantum wizardry powering our digital world.

The Quantum Future

Venturing into the quantum future, where quantum computing and AI converge, is akin to embarking on an expedition to explore a new dimension. This uncharted territory, where the traditional rules of computation no longer apply, promises a landscape teeming with unimaginable discoveries and possibilities. Imagine this fusion of technologies as embarking on a journey not just to a new country but to an entirely new dimension, where the fundamental laws of physics as we know them are rewritten.

In this future, quantum computing acts as a supercharger for AI, turbocharging its processing and learning speeds beyond our wildest dreams. It's as if AI, already a high-performance vehicle in the realm of computing, is suddenly equipped with a quantum engine, allowing it to soar to new heights of efficiency and capability. This isn't just a minor upgrade; it's a transformation that redefines what's possible, turning science fiction into science fact.

The potential of quantum AI is akin to exploring a new dimension, where the obstacles that once seemed insurmountable are now easily navigated. Complex problems such as climate modeling, drug discovery, and traffic optimization, which require immense computational resources, could be solved in a fraction of the time. It's like having a map that not only guides us through the tricky terrain of data ethics but also reveals shortcuts and hidden pathways we never knew existed.

This quantum leap forward in AI capabilities could lead to advancements in personalized medicine, where treatments are tailored not just to the individual but to the unique molecular makeup of their condition. In the realm of environmental conservation, quantum AI could model complex ecosystems with unprecedented accuracy, identifying the most effective interventions to protect endangered species and habitats.

However, venturing into this new dimension also requires us to navigate the ethical and societal implications of such powerful technology. The balance between harnessing the potential of quantum AI and ensuring its responsible use is delicate. It demands a collective effort from scientists, ethicists, policymakers, and the public to ensure that this quantum future benefits all of humanity, not just a privileged few.

As we stand on the brink of this exciting frontier, the future of quantum computing and AI is not just about technological advancement but about expanding the horizons of human knowledge and capability. It's a journey that promises to take us into the heart of the unknown, armed with a map and compass of our ethical principles, ready to discover the wonders that await in the quantum future.

Chapter 9

AI Synergy: Connecting the Dots

Exploring the concept of interconnected AI systems unveils a future where collaborative intelligence becomes a cornerstone of technological advancement. Picture this scenario as a team of experts, each with a unique skill set, coming together to tackle complex problems more efficiently. This analogy shines a light on how interconnected AI systems can enhance problem-solving capabilities, much like a diverse team pooling their expertise to achieve a common goal.

Interconnected AI systems function similarly to a think tank composed of various specialists. Each AI system, or "specialist," brings its own area of expertise to the table. Some might excel in processing natural language, understanding human emotions, or predicting weather patterns, while others might be adept at solving mathematical equations or simulating complex physical phenomena. When these systems collaborate, they can complement each other's capabilities, leading to innovative solutions that would be challenging to achieve independently.

. . .

This collaborative potential of AI systems can revolutionize industries by enabling more comprehensive and holistic approaches to problem-solving. For instance, in healthcare, interconnected AI systems can combine the prowess of diagnostic algorithms, treatment recommendation systems, and patient monitoring tools to provide more personalized and effective care. Similarly, in environmental science, AI systems specializing in climate modeling, pollution tracking, and renewable energy optimization can work together to devise more impactful strategies for combating climate change.

The analogy of interconnected AI systems as a team of experts not only highlights their collaborative potential but also underscores the importance of diversity in AI development. Just as a team benefits from the varied perspectives and skills of its members, the AI ecosystem thrives on the integration of diverse algorithms and approaches. This diversity ensures that interconnected AI systems can tackle problems from multiple angles, leading to more robust and creative solutions.

As we look to the future, the prospect of AI systems working in concert opens up exciting possibilities. It's a vision of technology where the whole is indeed greater than the sum of its parts, and where AI's collective intelligence can drive progress in ways we're just beginning to imagine. With careful development and ethical considerations, interconnected AI systems have the potential to transform how we address the world's most pressing challenges, offering a glimpse into a future where collaborative intelligence is a key driver of innovation.

Real-World Applications

Delving into the world of AI, particularly when it comes to the concept of interconnected systems, conjures an image of a symphony orchestra, where each instrument, or AI, plays its part in harmony to create a beautiful, complex performance. This ensemble, where each AI brings a unique skill set, works together to solve problems more efficiently, showcasing the collaborative potential and real-world applications of AI systems across various sectors.

Imagine the healthcare sector, where interconnected AI systems harmonize like a well-conducted orchestra. One AI system specializes in diagnosing diseases through imaging, another in analyzing genetic data to predict vulnerabilities to certain conditions, and yet another in monitoring patient health in real-time through wearable technology. Together, they provide a comprehensive healthcare service that's far more efficient and personalized than any single system could offer on its own. It's as if the radiologist, geneticist, and general practitioner are working in perfect concert, each contributing their expertise to improve patient outcomes.

In environmental science, interconnected AI systems collaborate to tackle climate change. One system models climate patterns and predicts changes, another analyzes satellite data to monitor deforestation, and a third optimizes renewable energy sources. This collaborative effort is akin to different sections of an orchestra—wind, strings, and percussion—each playing their part to perform a symphony that could inspire change and drive action towards a more sustainable future.

The transportation sector benefits similarly from this orchestral AI arrangement. One AI manages traffic flow in real-time, another predicts maintenance needs for public transportation vehicles, and yet another optimizes routes for delivery services. Together, they create a symphony of efficiency, reducing congestion, minimizing downtime, and ensuring goods and people move smoothly and sustainably.

These examples highlight the transformative power of interconnected AI systems across diverse sectors. Like musicians in an orchestra who, despite playing different instruments, come together to create something greater than the sum of their parts, interconnected AI systems combine their unique capabilities to address complex challenges with unprecedented efficiency and creativity. This collaborative future, where AI systems work in concert to enhance our world, is not only exciting but also within our reach, promising solutions to some of our most pressing problems and opening the door to a world of possibilities previously unimagined.

The Power of AI Collaboration

Exploring the transformative potential of AI collaboration unveils a future where the collective power of interconnected AI systems can solve complex challenges more efficiently and innovatively. This concept can be likened to assembling a puzzle, where each AI, akin to an individual puzzle piece, is crucial to completing the picture. Just as a single puzzle piece might not reveal much on its own, an individual AI system has limitations in what it can achieve independently. However, when these systems work together, sharing data, insights, and learning from each other, they form a complete, coherent picture that solves complex problems with unprecedented precision and efficiency.

In the real world, this collaborative approach is already beginning to take shape across various sectors, demonstrating the immense potential of interconnected AI systems. In healthcare, for example, AI collaboration is enabling more accurate diagnoses and personalized treatment plans by integrating data from genomics, medical imaging, and patient health records. This holistic view, much like a completed puzzle, provides a deeper understanding of patient health, leading to better outcomes.

In environmental conservation, interconnected AI systems are working together to monitor ecosystems, predict the impacts of climate change, and develop sustainable solutions. By pooling data from satellite imagery, climate models, and biodiversity research, these AI "puzzle pieces" provide a comprehensive picture of environmental health and help formulate strategies to protect our planet.

In the realm of urban planning and smart cities, AI collaboration is optimizing traffic flow, enhancing public safety, and improving energy efficiency. Different AI systems analyze data from traffic cameras, weather reports, and energy grids, working together to create more livable, sustainable urban environments.

The analogy of a symphony orchestra, where each AI plays its part in harmony, underscores the beauty and complexity of AI collaboration. Just as an orchestra's music is richer and more nuanced than any single instrument playing alone, the collaborative efforts of AI systems yield solutions that are more comprehensive, effective, and innovative than what could be achieved in isolation.

Looking to the future, the potential of AI collaboration is boundless. As these systems become more advanced and interconnected, we can expect to see even greater achievements in tackling some of the world's most pressing challenges. The key to unlocking this potential lies in continued innovation, ethical considerations, and a commitment to harnessing the power of AI for the greater good. With each AI system contributing its unique capabilities to the collective effort, the possibilities are as limitless as the number of pieces in the most complex puzzle imaginable.

Chapter 10

The Future of Software and AI Agents

E xploring the concept of AI-generated custom software solutions is like imagining a world where a personal chef can magically craft meals tailored exactly to your taste and nutritional needs. This chef doesn't just cook for you; they understand your preferences, allergies, and even your cravings at any given moment. Similarly, AI's potential to create personalized software solutions promises to revolutionize the way we think about and interact with technology.

In this enthusiastic dive into the future, let's consider AI as this personal chef in the realm of software development. Just as a chef combines ingredients in precise ways to create a delicious dish, AI can combine codes, algorithms, and user inputs to develop software that perfectly fits the unique requirements of each individual or business. Imagine a scenario where you need a specific application for your startup. Instead of sifting through off-the-shelf software that only meets some of your needs, you describe what you're looking for to an AI system. Like discussing your dietary preferences with a chef, you tell the AI about your business processes, your goals, and the challenges you're facing.

With this information, the AI goes to work, "cooking up" a software solution designed just for you. It selects the right "ingredients"—technologies, frameworks, and algorithms—and combines them in a way that's optimized for your specific use case. The result is a piece of custom software that fits your business like a glove, or a meal that's been tailored to satisfy your exact cravings.

The possibilities for this kind of AI collaboration in software development are vast. For individuals, it could mean apps that adapt to their learning style for education, or fitness programs that adjust in real-time based on performance and feedback. For businesses, it could lead to bespoke solutions for data analysis, customer relationship management, or even predictive maintenance for manufacturing processes, all designed with the specific nuances of the business in mind.

The concept of AI as a personal chef for software development is not just a playful speculation but a glimpse into a future where technology adapts to us, rather than the other way around. As AI continues to evolve, the potential for custom software on demand could transform our interaction with technology, making it more personal, efficient, and aligned with our individual needs and goals. Just as no two meals prepared by a personal chef are the same, no two software solutions created by AI would be identical, opening up a world of personalized technology that can grow and evolve with us.

The Rise of AI Agents

Diving into the future of personal AI assistants, let's unleash our imagination and envisage these AI agents as genies in digital bottles, poised to fulfill our digital wishes with just a command. This playful speculation on the development and impact of personal AI assistants highlights not just the convenience they could bring to our daily lives, but also the touch of whimsy in having such a powerful helper at our beck and call.

Imagine, for a moment, an AI agent designed to understand you better than you understand yourself. It knows your schedule, preferences, quirks, and even your coffee order. This isn't just a tool; it's a companion, ready to navigate the complexities of the digital world on your behalf. Like a genie granting wishes, these AI agents could make seemingly impossible tasks happen with a simple command, transforming the mundane into the magical.

The potential applications for such AI agents are as vast as they are exciting. In the realm of productivity, an AI agent could manage your emails, schedule your meetings, and even remind you to take a break, all while optimizing your workflow. It's like having a personal secretary who's not only incredibly efficient but also knows the best jokes.

In the realm of personal health, imagine an AI genie that monitors your fitness levels, suggests personalized workouts, and even motivates you with personalized pep talks. This agent would not just be an app on your phone but a partner in your journey to better health, adapting its recommendations based on your progress and preferences.

The entertainment possibilities are equally thrilling. Your personal AI agent could curate playlists, book recommendations, and even TV show suggestions based on your mood and past likes and dislikes. It's as if Netflix, Spotify, and Goodreads had a baby that could read your mind.

Of course, with great power comes great responsibility. The development of such personal AI agents will require careful consideration of privacy, ethics, and security. Ensuring these AI genies are used for good, respecting user data, and protecting against misuse will be paramount.

As we look to the future, the rise of personal AI agents offers a glimpse into a world where technology not only makes our lives easier but also adds a layer of enchantment to our daily routines. So, here's to the future of AI collaboration, where our digital genies are ready to make our wishes come true, one command at a time.

Personalization and Privacy

Addressing the delicate balance between personalized AI experiences and privacy concerns conjures the analogy of a diary with a lock. This diary, representing personal data, holds the secrets, wishes, and day-to-day details of its owner, accessible only to those granted permission. Similarly, as AI technologies evolve to offer increasingly customized experiences, they delve into the depths of personal data, necessitating a level of protection and respect akin to that of a locked diary.

The promise of personalized AI is akin to having a personal assistant who knows your preferences, anticipates your needs, and makes life more convenient and enjoyable. However, this level of personalization requires access to a wealth of personal information, from browsing habits to location data and even personal conversations. Just as one wouldn't leave a diary open for anyone to read, there's a growing need to ensure that personal data used by AI is safeguarded with utmost care.

Reflecting on this, the key lies in finding a middle ground where AI can still deliver personalized experiences without overstepping the boundaries of privacy. This requires transparent communication about what data is collected, how it's used, and the measures in place to protect it. Think of it as a diary that only opens with a key that the owner willingly provides, under the assurance that their secrets remain safe.

Moreover, just as a diary can be a source of insight and growth, so too can personal data, when used ethically, drive innovations that benefit the individual and society at large. The challenge is ensuring that these innovations do not come at the cost of individual privacy and autonomy.

In this reflective exploration, the analogy of a diary with a lock serves as a reminder of the value of personal data and the importance of protecting it in the age of AI. As we navigate the complexities of personalization and privacy, it's crucial to maintain a dialogue that prioritizes the rights and dignity of individuals, ensuring that the future of AI remains both bright and respectful of the personal boundaries it seeks to understand.

Chapter 11

The Double-Edged Sword: Voice Cloning and Deepfakes

Exploring the technology behind voice cloning and deepfake technologies is akin to unveiling the secrets of a skilled mask maker, crafting digital representations so accurate they can fool even the keenest audience. This journey into the mechanics of such technology is both informative and engaging, aiming to demystify the processes that enable such eerily lifelike digital creations.

Voice cloning technology, at its core, involves analyzing a target voice's unique characteristics—its pitch, tone, modulation, and even the subtlest of inflections. This process is similar to an artist studying the minute details of a face to craft a mask that perfectly captures its essence. By feeding these vocal characteristics into sophisticated AI algorithms, the technology synthesizes and reproduces a voice that can mimic the original speaker with astonishing accuracy. It's as if the AI becomes a ventriloquist, able to throw its voice in such a way that the listener is convinced the sound is coming from the original source.

· · ·

Deepfake technology, on the other hand, takes this artistry to the visual domain. It uses advanced machine learning techniques, particularly those involving generative adversarial networks (GANs), to superimpose one person's face onto another in video or still images. The process can be likened to a mask maker who not only crafts a mask that looks like the target but also ensures it moves and reacts in a way that mimics the real person's expressions and emotions. This technology analyses countless images or video frames of the target, learning how to recreate their facial movements so accurately that the resulting deepfake video can pass as genuine to the untrained eye.

Both voice cloning and deepfake technologies showcase the remarkable capabilities of AI to recreate and simulate reality with precision. However, like the work of a skilled mask maker, the use of these technologies comes with significant ethical considerations. The potential for misuse in creating misleading or harmful content means that, while we marvel at the technological prowess behind these digital masks, we must also navigate the moral landscape they inhabit with caution and responsibility.

In essence, as we delve into the technology behind the mask, we are reminded of the power of AI to blur the lines between reality and simulation. It invites us to question not only what we see and hear but also the implications of such technology in our digital age. As we look forward to the advancements in AI, it's crucial to balance our enthusiasm for innovation with a commitment to ethical use, ensuring that the digital masks we create serve to enrich our understanding of the world rather than distort it.

Potential for Misuse

Addressing the ethical concerns and potential misuse of deepfake technology involves a serious yet accessible discussion, akin to highlighting the danger of a wolf in sheep's clothing. This technology, capable of disguising misinformation as truth, represents a significant challenge in the digital age, requiring vigilance and ethical consideration.

Deepfake technology, by manipulating audio and video to create seemingly real content, acts much like a mask maker who crafts eerily accurate masks. However, unlike traditional masks worn for entertainment or art, these digital masks can be used to spread falsehoods, manipulate public opinion, and undermine trust in media. The analogy of a wolf in sheep's clothing aptly illustrates the potential for deepfakes to harm individuals and society by presenting malicious intent as benign or truthful content.

The sophistication of deepfake technology means that distinguishing between genuine and manipulated content is becoming increasingly difficult for the average person. This blurring of lines between reality and fabrication poses a threat not only to individual reputations but also to the foundational trust upon which democratic societies rely. Just as a shepherd must be vigilant to protect the flock from wolves in disguise, society must develop tools, regulations, and awareness to guard against the misuse of deepfakes.

Efforts to combat the negative impacts of deepfake technology include developing detection tools that can identify manipulated content, promoting digital literacy to educate the public about the existence and nature of deepfakes, and implementing legal and policy measures to penalize the malicious use of this technology. Like a lock on a diary, these measures aim to protect the integrity of personal and public discourse in the digital realm.

In conclusion, while deepfake technology showcases the remarkable capabilities of AI and machine learning, it also underscores the urgent need for ethical guidelines, awareness, and protective measures. By approaching this challenge with a clear understanding of the risks and a commitment to ethical technology use, society can hope to mitigate the dangers posed by digital wolves in sheep's clothing, ensuring that the digital future remains secure and trustworthy.

Fighting Back

Delving into the strategies to detect and combat deepfakes brings an optimistic lens to the technological and societal defenses available to us. The effort to safeguard against misinformation can be likened to the meticulous work of a detective unraveling disguises to reveal the truth. In this analogy, deepfake technology is akin to a sophisticated disguise, capable of cloaking falsehoods as credible information. Our "detectives"—comprising AI researchers, technologists, and informed citizens—are equipped with advanced tools and knowledge to peel away these digital disguises and expose the underlying fabrications.

On the technological front, innovations in machine learning and digital forensics are leading the charge against deepfakes. These tools scrutinize videos and audio recordings for inconsistencies invisible to the human eye, such as irregular blinking patterns or unnatural lip movements. It's akin to our detectives wielding magnifying glasses that reveal hidden clues within the digital noise.

Legislative and policy measures act as the rulebook guiding our detectives. By establishing clear legal frameworks around the creation and distribution of deepfakes, societies can deter malicious use. These laws serve as the detective's code of conduct, delineating what is permissible in the pursuit of truth and what crosses the line into deception.

Public awareness and education are pivotal in this fight. Just as a detective educates the public on how to protect themselves from scams, raising awareness about deepfakes empowers individuals to critically assess the content they consume. Workshops, public campaigns, and educational programs can equip people with the skills to spot signs of manipulated content, transforming each viewer into a savvy detective in their own right.

Collaborative efforts underscore the battle against deepfakes as a collective endeavor involving governments, tech companies, and civil society. This collaboration ensures that as deepfake technology evolves, so too do our methods of detection and defense. This global detective agency, through shared knowledge and resources, amplifies our collective ability to protect the integrity of information.

In this optimistic view, the fight against deepfakes is an ongoing journey blending technology, law, and education. By equipping our detectives with the best tools, rules, and knowledge, we can unmask the falsehoods and safeguard the truth, ensuring that the digital world remains a space for genuine expression and informed discourse.

Chapter 12

The Art of Prompt Engineering

Diving into the art of creating effective prompts for AI is akin to crafting the perfect coffee order that ensures you get exactly what you want, every time. This playful and insightful exploration sheds light on the artistry behind prompts, illustrating how precise communication can lead to desired outcomes.

Crafting a prompt for AI is similar to ordering your favorite coffee concoction. Just as you'd specify your drink with precision—perhaps a "large latte with almond milk, two shots of espresso, and a dash of cinnamon"—creating an effective prompt involves detailing exactly what you need from the AI. This specificity guides the AI, much like a barista, to deliver the desired result without confusion.

The analogy extends to understanding the nuances of the "ingredients" at your disposal. Just as you might customize your coffee order based on your mood, the time of day, or your dietary preferences, tailoring prompts for AI requires an understanding of the available tools, language models, and how they can be combined to address your specific needs.

Moreover, just as a barista might ask clarifying questions to ensure they make your coffee order to your liking, iterative refinement of prompts through feedback loops with AI can enhance the clarity and effectiveness of the interaction. This process of adjustment and learning mirrors the way we refine our coffee orders over time to better suit our tastes.

In essence, the art of prompt engineering is about mastering the language and structure of communication with AI to achieve outcomes that are as satisfying as a perfectly crafted cup of coffee. It requires a blend of creativity, precision, and a deep understanding of the capabilities and limitations of AI technologies. As we become more adept at crafting these prompts, we unlock the full potential of AI to assist, innovate, and inspire in ways that are tailored perfectly to our individual needs and aspirations.

The Demand for Prompt Engineers

The emerging job market for prompt engineers can be likened to a modern gold rush, where possessing the right skills and insights can uncover vast opportunities within the AI landscape. This burgeoning field, niche yet rapidly growing, represents a frontier of technological exploration and innovation.

Prompt engineering is the craft of designing and refining the inputs given to AI models to elicit the desired outputs. This skill set is akin to finding the most effective way to communicate with a genie, ensuring that your wishes are understood and granted precisely as intended. Just as prospectors during the gold rush needed to know where to dig and how to sift through the silt to find nuggets of gold, prompt engineers must navigate the complexities of language models, understanding how to phrase prompts to tap into the AI's capabilities fully.

The demand for these skills is driven by the increasing reliance on AI across various sectors, from customer service and content creation to more specialized fields like legal analysis and medical research. Organizations are seeking individuals who can not only interact with AI effectively but also innovate in the way AI is applied to solve problems and generate value. This has opened up a new vein of professional opportunity for those who can bridge the gap between human intention and AI comprehension.

The rise of prompt engineers is reflective of the broader trend towards more sophisticated AI applications, necessitating a deeper understanding of how to communicate with and guide these systems. Like the miners who were equipped with the tools and knowledge to extract precious metals, prompt engineers are armed with linguistic acuity, technical understanding, and creative thinking, making them invaluable in the AI-driven economy.

This field is not just about technical proficiency but also about understanding the nuances of human communication and how these can be translated into a form that AI can process and act upon. The role of a prompt engineer, therefore, is not unlike that of a translator or interpreter, converting human desires and questions into a language that AI can understand and respond to effectively.

As we venture further into this AI gold rush, the skills of prompt engineering will become increasingly critical, offering a path to those who wish to explore the untapped potential of AI collaboration. With a blend of technical knowledge, linguistic skill, and creative thinking, prompt engineers stand at the forefront of the AI frontier, shaping the future of how we interact with and benefit from intelligent systems.

Best Practices and Pitfalls

Exploring the nuances of crafting effective prompts for AI is akin to navigating a maze where strategic choices lead directly to the treasure while cleverly avoiding traps. This journey is both playful and insightful, shedding light on the artistry behind prompt engineering—a field that's quickly becoming indispensable in the AI-driven world.

Crafting an effective prompt is much like plotting a course through a maze. The goal is to navigate through complex pathways (the AI's processing capabilities) to reach the desired outcome efficiently. Just as a maze runner might use clues and markers to avoid dead ends, a prompt engineer uses specific language and structure to guide the AI towards generating the desired output. This precision in communication ensures that the AI understands the task at hand, much like a well-drawn map helps a maze runner visualize their route to the treasure.

A common pitfall in this process is ambiguity. Just as vague directions can lead a maze runner into a trap, an unclear prompt can lead AI down the wrong path, resulting in outputs that miss the mark. The key to avoiding this is specificity—clearly defining the task, context, and expected outcome in the prompt. This clarity acts as a beacon, guiding the AI through the complexity of its neural networks towards the correct solution.

Another important practice is iterative refinement. Much like a maze runner might backtrack and try a different path upon hitting a dead end, prompt engineers should be prepared to refine their prompts based on the AI's responses. This iterative process ensures continuous improvement and learning, optimizing the path to success with each attempt.

Moreover, understanding the AI's limitations is crucial, akin to recognizing the boundaries and rules of the maze. Just as a runner wouldn't attempt to climb over the maze walls, prompt engineers must work within the capabilities and constraints of the AI model they're interacting with. This understanding allows for more realistic expectations and more effective prompts.

In summary, crafting the perfect prompt for AI is an art that requires precision, clarity, and an understanding of the AI's capabilities. By viewing prompt engineering through the lens of navigating a maze, we can appreciate the strategic thinking and creativity involved in guiding AI to generate useful and accurate outputs. With these best practices in mind, we can avoid common pitfalls and unlock the full potential of AI to serve our needs.

Afterword

As we draw this journey to its close, we extend our heartfelt gratitude for choosing our book as your guide to navigating the transformative world of AI. Your decision to embark on this learning path with us is deeply appreciated.

The landscape of artificial intelligence is vast and ever-changing, akin to navigating uncharted waters. We hope that through the pages of this book, we've provided you with a compass and map to steer by, demystifying complex concepts and spotlighting the opportunities AI brings to our world.

If this book has enlightened, inspired, or aided you in any way, we kindly ask that you consider leaving a review wherever you purchased it. Your feedback is not only valuable to us but also helps others discover the insights and knowledge shared within these pages.

Thank you once again for allowing us to be a part of your journey into the world of artificial intelligence. As the AI landscape continues to evolve, may you remain curious, adaptable, and always forward-looking, ready to embrace the myriad opportunities that lie ahead.

82